OF THE TOWN OF

METHUEN,

FROM ITS

SETTLEMENT TO THE YEAR 1876.

BY JOS. S. HOWE.

METHUEN, MASS.:
E. L. HOUGHTON & CO., PRINTERS, CURRIER'S BUILDING, BROADWAY.
1876.

HISTORICAL SKETCH

OF THE TOWN OF

METHUEN,

FROM ITS

SETTLEMENT TO THE YEAR 1876.

BY JOS. S. HOWE.

METHUEN, MASS.:
E. L. HOUGHTON & CO., PRINTERS, CURRIER'S BUILDING, BROADWAY.
1876.

HISTORICAL SKETCH.

It is not attempted in the following pages to present a complete history of the Town of Methuen. The limited time for preparation of this Sketch only admits a recital of the principal facts. No attempt to write the early history of this town has ever been made, and as the old times recede, and old people drop into their graves, much valuable material is becoming lost forever. The investigation necessary to prepare this paper has shown, that by proper effort many old traditions, and much valuable information, might be gathered which would be of great interest and value, not only to us, but to those who come after us. At present, however, we must be content with a rapid and imperfect statement of some of the principal facts in our history as a town.

The native inhabitants of the valley of the Merrimack were the Penacook or Pawtucket Indians, of whom the Chief was Passaconnaway, always a firm friend of the settlers. These were subdivided into smaller tribes. The Agawams had their home on the coast, from the Merrimack to Cape Ann; the Wamesits at the junction of the Concord and Merrimack rivers (Lowell); the Pentuckets at the mouth of "Little river," in Haverhill; but no evidence appears showing that any particular Indian tribe had its home in Methuen. It is certain, however, that Bodwell's falls (at the Lawrence dam,) and the shores of the Spicket as far as "Spicket falls," were favorite resorts of the Indians, especially during the fishing season. The rivers in those early days, and for many years afterwards, swarmed with salmon, shad, alewives, bass and sturgeon. The salmon was the principal fish used as food; the shad and alewives were used by the Indians to manure their corn, and their example was followed by the settlers. It is said on good authority that it was no unusual thing to specify in the articles of agreement between master and apprentice that the apprentice should not be required to eat salmon above six times a week.

Some years before the first settlement of the country, a violent war broke out among the Indians, which resulted in the destruction of a large number. This was succeeded by a pestilence, which carried off many more, so that the number of Indians found by the first settlers in this region was very small. The greater part of Methuen was at first included in the town of Haverhill. That town was first settled in 1640 by about a dozen colonists from Newbury, headed by Mr. Nathaniel Ward. Two years after, the whole territory was purchased of the Indians, Passaquo and Saggahew, who are supposed to have been among the last of the Pentuckets. The original deed—of which the following is a copy—is now in possession of the city of Haverhill:

"KNOW ALL MEN BY THESE PRESENTS, that we, Passaquo and Saggahew, with ye consent of Passaconnaway: have sold unto ye inhabitants of Pentuckett all ye lands we have in Pentuckett; that is eyght myles in length from ye little Rivver in Pentuckett. Westward; Six myles in length from ye aforesaid Rivver northward; And six myles in length from ye foresaid Rivver Eastward, with ye Ileand and ye rivver that ye ileand stand in as far in length as ye land lyes by as formerly expressed: that is fourteen myles in length;

And wee ye said Passaquo and Sagga Hew with ye consent of Passaconnaway, have sold unto ye said inhabitants all ye right that wee or any of us have in ye said ground and Ileand and Rivver;

And we warrant it against all or any other Indians whatsoever unto ye said Inhabitants of Pentuckett, and to their heirs and assigns forever. Dated ye fifteenth day of november Ann Dom 1642.

Witness our hands and seales to this bargayne of sale ye day and year above written (in ye presents of us) we ye said Passaquo & Sagga Hew have received in hand, for & in consideration of ye same three pounds & ten shillings.

JOHN WARD,
ROBERT CLEMENTS,
TRISTRAM COFFIN,
HUGH SHERRATT,
WILLIAM WHITE,
ye sign of (1)
THOMAS DAVIS.

PASSAQUO YE MARKE OF (a bow and arrow) PASSAQUO. [SEAL]

SAGGA HEW YE MARKE OF (a bow and arrow) SAGGA HEW. [SEAL]

It is not easy to see exactly what the Indians intended to convey by this deed, nor does it appear to have been clear to the early settlers; for no regular survey was made until 1666, when we find that a committee was appointed by the General Court to "run the bounds of the Town of Haverhill." They began at the meeting-house, which was situated about half a mile east of Little river, and ran due west eight miles and "reared a heap of stones" (which point must have been a mile or two west of Salem village). Then they ran from that heap of stones due south until they touched the Merrimack (somewhere near the island east of the Bartlett farm), and north until they struck the northern line of the town.

This western boundary of the town remained unchanged until Methuen was set off sixty years afterwards. As finally determined the shape of the town of Haverhill was triangular. Starting from Holt's Rock ("Rocks Village,") the line ran due northwest until it met the north and south line from Merrimack River, as mentioned above.

The strip of land, perhaps a mile and a half in width, between Haverhill Line and "Drawcut" line seems to have been granted by the General Court to individuals. An old plan in the County records indicates that Major Denison, who had a grant of 600 acres from the General Court in 1660, owned more than a thousand acres on the river, above the Haverhill line, including what is now the Bartlett farm and lands south and west. West of that was Col. Higginson's farm of over three hundred acres. A little north of these was Marshall Michelson's tract of three hundred acres. Printer Green had three hundred acres lying on each side of the brook which runs from "White's pond," then called "North pond."

Thus it will be seen that the title to a great portion of the land in Methuen came directly from the aboriginal owners. It is said that the uplands at that time were mostly covered by a heavy growth of timber, except an occasional spot burned over by fires set by the Indians. The meadows were, many of them, cleared and covered with a tall and dense growth of grass. The Indians were accustomed to burn the grass in the fall, that they might more easily capture the deer resorting to them to feed on the young grass in the spring. These meadows appear to have been much sought after by the early settlers, who obtained from them, the principal subsistence for their cattle. They cut and stacked the hay in the summer and in the winter drew it home on sleds. An early writer says of Haverhill: "The people are wholly bent to improve their labor in tilling the earth and keeping of cattel whose yearly increase encourages them to spend their days in those remote parts. The constant penetrating further into this Wilderness hath caused the wild and uncouth wood to be filled with frequented ways, and the large rivers to be overlaid with Bridges passable both for horse and foot; this town is of large extent, there being an overweaning desire in most men after meadow land," &c. The records of the town of Haverhill show that no one was admitted to the rights and privileges of the Colony unless first voted in by the town.

The lands were divided among the inhabitants in accordance with a vote "That he who had £200 should have 20 acres for his house lot, and every one under that sum to have acres proportioned for his house lot, together with meadow and common and planting ground proportionally."

Lot-layers were chosen by the town to divide the land among the inhabitants as it was cleared up or became accessible. From this mode of division it happened that one man would own a large number of small lots scattered over the whole town. It is now very difficult to exactly locate the lots as they are recorded in the Haverhill records, because they were usually bounded only by marked trees. These descriptions show that some of our local names were of very ancient date. In 1673, thirty-two acres of land were laid off to John Clements, bounded by "Sowes brook." In 1678, "eleven score acres of upland" were laid off to James Davis, Sen., bounded on the west by Spicket river, Spicket falls being the southwest bound. In 1683, we find the record of a similar lot lying on the southerly side, running to "Bloody brook" on the east, and taken up by James Davis, Jr. These lots included the land now occupied by the east part of Methuen village.

In 1658, five acres of meadow were laid off in "Strongwater" near a "little pond." In 1666, a parcel of meadow was laid out to Matthias Button, on the south side of "Spicket hill." In 1659, there was a division of the land west of the Spicket river, with a provision that "if more than two acres meadow be found on any one lot it shall remain to the town." In the same year we find a record of the laying off three acres of land in "Mistake meadow" in the west part of Haverhill, whence we conclude the name originated in somebody's blunder, and by some mistake has become "Mystic." The distribution of common lands was continued from time to time, until finally, after much contention between the old settlers and new comers, the "Proprietors," or owners of the common land, organized separately from the town and disposed of the remaining land as they saw fit. Our townsman, David Nevins, Esq., has in his possession a grant from the "proprietors," of the islands in the Spicket above the falls, to Asa and Robert Swan, for £2 10 shillings, and bearing the date of 1721.

We can find no record showing when the first settlement was made within the present limits of Methuen, or who made it. It is certain that the east and south parts of the town near the river, were first occupied, doubtless because they were nearer the villages of Haverhill and Andover. We have been informed by Asa Simonds, Esq., that when repairing the old "Bodwell house"—now in Lawrence—some years ago, a brick was found bearing the date 1660, which had been marked upon it before the brick was burnt. This would seem to indicate that a house was built in the neighborhood near that date.

It is not unlikely that further inquiry may fix the date and place of the first settlements here with considerable certainty. It seems doubtful whether there were many settlers in Methuen until near the time it was set off from Haverhill. It is likely that the Indian troubles which extended over many years previous to 1720, seriously checked, if they did not entirely prevent, the settlement on farms. Andover and Haverhill were made frontier towns by act of General Court and both towns suffered severely during the Indian war. But we have never seen a record of an Indian attack on settlers living upon territory which afterwards became Methuen. There were many attacks on the scattered settlers in West Haverhill and in Andover, and if there had been many inhabitants in Methuen, it is hardly probable that the Indians would have passed them by. There are some old traditions of encounters with the Indians, in this town, which we have not space to relate. The most important of these events took place in Feb. 1698; Jonathan Haynes and Samuel Ladd with their two sons had been to London meadow from their homes, in West Haverhill, for hay, each with a team consisting of a pair of oxen and a horse. The path lay along betwen Howe street and World's End pond. When returning home, just northeast of the pond, they were suddenly set upon by a party of Indians who had concealed themselves in the bushes on each side of the path. These Indians, fourteen in number, were returning from Andover where they had killed and captured several persons. They killed Haynes and Ladd with their hatchets, took one of the boys prisoner and kept him for some years; the other boy cut one of the horses loose, jumped on his back and got away. The Indians then killed the oxen, took out their tongues and the best pieces and went on their way. We find no record of trouble with the Indians after 1708.

In 1712, nine persons living in that part of Haverhill now Methuen, petitioned the town to abate their rates for the support of the ministry and schools, and the town voted to abate one-half their taxes. In 1722, a petition was presented to the town of Haverhill by persons living in what is now Methuen, to be set off as a separate town or parish. This petition was not granted. The next year Joshua Swan and 26 others, with shrewd foresight, petitioned the Town of Haverhill to "set off fifty or sixty acres of land southwest of Bare meadow, together with a piece of land lying on a hill commonly called Meeting-house hill in times past, reserved by our forefathers for the use of the ministry, might in hard times make a convenient parsonage, if by the blessing of God the Gospel might so flourish amongst us, and we grow so prosperous as to be able to maintain and carry on the Gospel ministry amongst us." This petition was granted at the next town meeting, but it did not serve to make the petitioners less intent on a separation. Soon after, Lieut. Stephen Barker and other inhabitants of the western part of Haverhill, petitioned the General Court for an act to incorporate them into a new town. The act passed in December, 1725, and was as follows:

"An act for Dividing the Town of Haverhill and erecting a new Town there and in parts adjacent, by the name of Methuen. Whereas the West part of the Town of Haverhill within the County of Essex, and parts adjacent not included within any Township is Competently filled with Inhabitants, who labor under great Difficulties by their remoteness from the place of Publick Worship, &c., and they having made their application to this Court that they may be set off a distinct and separate Town and be vested with all the Powers and Privileges of a Town. Be it therefore enacted by the Lieutenant Governor, Council and Representatives in General Court assembled and by the authority of the same. That the West part of the said Town of Haverhill with the land adjoining be, and hereby are set off and constituted a separate Township by the name of Methuen, the bounds of the said Township to be as follows, viz:— Beginning at the mouth of Hawkes' Meadow Brook, so called, in Merrimack River, and from thence to run half a point to the northward of the northwest to an heap of stones, or till it intersect Haverhill line; from thence upon a straight course to the head of Dunstable line, and so upon Dracut line about four miles to a pine southeast. frome thence six miles or thereabouts upon Dracut line, South to Merrimack River, and from thence to run down said river ten mile and forty pole till it come to the first mentioned bounds. And that the inhabitants of the said lands as before described and bounded, be and hereby are invested with the Powers, Priviliges and Immunities that the Inhabitants of any of the towns of this Province by law are or ought to be vested with.

Provided, That the Inhabitants of the said Town of Methuen, do within the space of Three Years from the Publication of this Act, erect and finish a suitable house for the Publick Worship of God, and procure and settle a Learned, Orthodox minister of good conversation and make provision for his comfortable and honorable support, and that they set apart a lot of Two Hundred arces of land in some convenient Place in the said Town, for the use of the ministry, and a lot of fifty acres for the use of a School. And that thereupon they be discharged from any further payments for the maintenance of the ministry in Haverhill. And be it further enacted by the authority aforesaid, That the Inhabitants of the said Town of Methuen, be and and hereby are empowered to assess all the lands of Non Residents lying within the said town, Two pence per acre towards the building of the Meeting House, and settling of a minister there. Provided, nevertheless that there be and hereby is made a Reservation or Saving of the Right and property of the Province Lands (if any there be) within the bounds aforesaid, to this Province."

It was ordered by the Court "that Mr. Stephen Barker, a principal inhabitant of the Town of Methuen be, and hereby is empowered and directed to notifie and summons the inhabitants of the said town duly qualified for voters, to assemble and meet sometime in the month of March next, to choose town officers according to law, to stand for the year." In compliance with this order a meeting was appointed for the ninth of March. The following is a copy of the record of that first town meeting held in Methuen :

"Att our first annual meeting in the town of methuen, march ye 9th 1725,6 Leutanent Stephen Barker was leaguly chosen moderator for ye meeting.

Att the same meeting william whittier was chosen town clark & sworn for ye yer insewing.

Att the same meeting selectmen war leaguly chosen for ye year.

1	JOHN BAILEY,	Select men sworn
2	EBENEZER BARKER,	to the faithful discharg
3	ASIE SWAN,	of the ofies of assesers
4	DANIEL BODWEL,	august ye second 1726
5	THOMAS WHITTIER.	before me William Whittier
		town clark.

att ye same meeting Richard swan is leaguly chosen cunstable for the year insewing.

voted that the cunstable or colector shall be paid one shilling for each twenty shillings of money that he shall colect or gather of the Taxes which shall be laied upon the nonrazedance or peopel which belong to other towns. March ye 9th 1725,6 the toun voated that Thomas silver should be excepted to serve cunstable or colector instead of Richard swan for ye year insewing and ye same day thomas silver was sworn to the fathfull discharge of the office of a cunstable by the selectmen of methuen. Robert swan is leaguly chosen town treasurer att the same meeting march ye 9 for ye year insewing. town treasurer sworn.

Serveirs of high ways.
1 ROBERT SWAN,
2 EPHRAIM CLARK,
3 BENJAMIN STEPHENS,
4 THOMAS MASSER.
of highwaye serveirs all sworn.

fence vewers JOHN I. CROSS,
SAMUELL STEPHENS. 2 Both sworn.

Tithen men 1 JAMES HOW,
2 WILLIAM GUTTERSON. Both tithen sworn.
field drivers 1 JOHN HASTINGS,
2 ZEBADIAH AUSTING.

att the same meeting March ye 9 1725,6 hoge riefs was leaguly chosen
SAMUEL SMITH
THOMAS AUSTING
hog riefs Both sworn.

Att ye same meeting march ye 9 voted yt hogs should go att large acording to law.

Att a town meeting march ye 9 1725,6.

Voted that the select men should have power to a gree with an athadoxt minester to serve in the work of the minestry for ye year insewing and not to exceed five and forty pownds and find the minester his diat.

So far as we can learn, no other town in the country bears the name of "Methuen." How this name originated has been a matter of considerable speculation. Some have thought that it took its name from a town in Scotland called "Methven," and others have supposed that this town was named in honor of Lord Methven of Scotland. A. C. Goodell, Esq., of Salem, who is engaged in preparing the Provincial Laws for publication, suggests a theory which we think must be the true one. It was a common thing in those days, when a town was incorporated, for the Governor to give it a name. The act of incorporation was passed by the Legislature, engrossed and sent to the Governor, with a space for the name in blank. When it was presented for his signature, he inserted the name in the proper place.

The original act of Incorporation of the Town of Methuen, in the office of the Secretary of State, clearly shows that the name was inserted by a hand different from the one that engrossed the bill. The act is written upon the parchment in a large, full hand, while the name is written in a small, running hand, and with ink of a different color, but similar to that used by Gov. Dummer in writing his signature.

A careful examination of the writing leaves little doubt that Gov. Dummer wrote the name with his own hand when he attached his signature. Of course it is now impossible to give with certainty the reason which suggested the name to him. But at that time there was one Lord Paul Methuen who was Privy Councellor to the King, and who was for some years prominent in the English Government. It is altogether likely that the town was named for him and it is also pretty certain that these facts are about all we can ever learn about it.

We find from the town records that nine town meetings were held during the first year, and that the principal business was locating the meeting-house and perfecting the necessary arrangements for religious service. At that time, and for many years after, the minister and meeting-house were supported by a town tax, as schools and highways are now.

Unfortunately at the outset, a bitter quarrel sprang up concerning the location of the meeting-house. On the 28th of May, 1726, a meeting was called to " prefix " a place whereon to build a meeting-house. Twenty-eight persons voted in favor of locating the house "between James Davis' and Samuel Smith's house" (Powder House hill,) twenty-two entered their "dissent against the meeting-house being carried from the meeting-house land, or hill so called,"—the land which had been granted by Haverhill two years before—and supported their "dissent" by a quaint and vigorous argument. The dispute waxed hot, meeting after meeting was held, votes to provide labor and material were carried and reconsidered, but the majority finally prevailed and the new meeting-house was raised and boarded on "Powder House hill." The minority, however, were determined not to be beaten, and petitioned the General Court to reverse the popular decision. The committee appointed by the Court to visit the place concluded that the parsonage lot "was the properest place for the meeting-house to stand," so the minority were victorious, and in May, 1727, the town voted to remove the frame to the "place where the Court ordered it should stand."

The town records show that the Sunday services, as well as the town meetings, were held at the house of Asie Swan until the meeting-house was ready for occupancy. Asie Swan seems to have been a man "prominent in those days" and his house is said to have been situated a little east of Prospect hill. The meeting-house was "forty feet long, thirty feet wide, and twenty feet stud." There was but one pew, and that for the minister's family, the congregation generally being seated on benches. There were no means of heating the house in cold weather, until within the recollection of persons now living, and in the cold winter mornings the humble worshippers must have needed a fiery discourse to make them comfortable. It is said that there was a tavern in those days on the "Frye place" to which the meeting goers usually resorted at noon, where they found a kettle of hot water ready, and plenty of *spiritual* comfort less etherial than that which they received within the sacred edifice.

The first road laid out by the Town of Methuen extended from somewhere on "Hawkes Meadow brook to James Howe's well," and was probably a part of Howe street north of the Taylor farm. The records of the Town of Haverhill show that previous to that time a large number of town ways had been laid out in the west part of the town—probably for convenience in reaching the meadows and woodland. At this distance of time it is almost impossible to trace them unless they happen to touch some well known point. They generally commence at a marked tree, by some path, thence to some other tree, thence to a stump marked, and finally come out at another path, and are almost invariably two rods wide.

The roads of those days were probably little better than an ordinary cart path in the woods. Occasionally we find a record of money paid to the owners of land over which a public way passed, but no money appears to have been paid by the town for building. In fact scarcely more than a path was necessary, for there were no vehicles but ox carts and sleds. People traveled on horseback and went to market with their goods in saddlebags. Indeed it is said by persons now living in the town that within their recollection there were no wagons of any kind, or pleasure carriages except a few chaises, which were introduced about the beginning of the century.

The Town of Methuen as originally set off, included a large part of Salem, N. H., and perhaps a part of Windham. There seems to have been a tract of land between Haverhill and Dracut not comprised within the limits of any town. This tract was added to that part of Haverhill set off to Methuen, making a town nearly as large as Haverhill after the division. In 1741, the line between Massachusetts and New Hampshire was fixed substantially as it now runs, three miles from Merrimack river, and parallel with it. We have often wondered why it was, that the parties who fixed the State line, did not either make the line straight, or make the river the dividing line. The facts seem to have been as follows: The charter first given to the Massachusetts colony granted "all that part of New England lying between three miles to the north of the Merrimack and three miles to the south of the Charles river and of every part thereof in the Massachusetts Bay; and in length between the described breadth from the Atlantic Ocean to the South Sea." Under the charter the Massachusetts colony claimed that their northern boundary was three miles to the north of the northernmost point of the Merrimack, and they fixed upon a rock near the outlet of Lake Winnipisseogee, as the most northern part of the river. This would give to Massachusetts a large part of Vermont and New Hampshire, and a large section in Maine. The New Hampshire grantees claimed that under the Massachusetts charter the line could not extend in any place more than three miles from the river. The territory between these lines became disputed ground concerning which there was constant contention. In 1720, the New Hampshire colonists modified their claim, so far as to propose that the line should begin at a point three miles north from the mouth of the Merrimack, and thence run due west to the South Sea. The Massachusetts Colony refused to agree to this, and the contention became more violent until finally the Legislatures of the two colonies met,—the New Hampshire Legislature at Hampton Falls, and the Massachusetts at Salisbury, for the purpose of settling the difficulty. They appointed committees of conference, but were unable to agree, and after several weeks of angry discussion the whole subject was referred to the King of England for decision. The matter was decided by the King in Council in 1740, and it was decreed that the northern boundary of the Province of Massachusetts

Bay, "is and be a similar curved line pursuing the curve of Merrimack River at three miles distance, on the north side thereof and beginning at the Atlantic Ocean."

This decree gave to New Hampshire seven hundred square miles more than she asked for, and a line crooked as the curve of the river. Tradition says that this decision was brought about by sharp practice on the part of the agent appointed by New Hampshire to lay the subject before the King. This boundary line has since remained unchanged. It cut off a large slice of the original territory of the town of Methuen, but it is not likely there were many inhabitants except in the neighborhood of "Spicket hill," where there must have been quite an important settlement.

The exact number of inhabitants at that time in the whole town is unknown. An old tax book among the town records, shows that the number of persons taxed in Methuen in 1740, was 165, of which 71 lived in that part of the town cut off by the New Hampshire line, and 85 in the present limits of Methuen.

The fact that strikes us most forcibly in reading over the early town records, is the prominence given to religious observances. The chief and only reason given for setting off the new town, was that the people might more easily attend the public worship of God. The first business done was to provide themselves a minister and place of public worship. Their principal money tax was for the support of these objects. Nothing could show more plainly that the hardy pioneers of Methuen were of genuine Puritan stock. Whatever we may think of Puritan austerity and fanaticism and intolerance, we cannot help admiring the indomitable energy, the iron will, and lofty purpose of these men who braved the dangers of hostile Indians and suffered the privations of the wilderness, that they might worship God in their own way. The old papers which have been preserved, the town records, and the old traditions, all show that the first settlers in Methuen were men of rugged, vigorous intellect, accustomed to think for themselves, and not afraid to express their opinions.

Our forefathers seem to have provided for the educational interests of the town at an early date. In 1733, we find that Ebenezer Barker, Zebediah Barker and Thomas Eaton were each paid £2 10s. for keeping school. In 1731, the town voted to keep school one month in Ebenezer Barker's house, one month in Thomas Eaton's and a month at Joshua Swan's. In 1735, the town voted to build a school-house 18x20 feet, near the meeting-house, school to be kept two months at the school-house and one month at Spicket hill. The school appears to have been kept at the school-house part of the time, but chiefly at private houses until 1792. Reading and writing and a little arithmetic were the principal branches taught, and the latter study was not required. The schools appear to have been taught by male teachers only until 1749, when it was voted "to choose schoolmistresses to instruct children in their reading. Also voted to choose a committee to agree with schoolmistresses and appoint convenient places for them to be kept in."

In 1775, the town was divided into seven school districts each of which was to have its proportion of the school money, provided it built a comfortable school-house. Up to that time the Selectmen usually had the sole care of the schools. Mr. David Nevins has in his possession the return made by the committee whose duty it was to build the school-houses, from which it appears that the building of them was let out at auction to the lowest bidder, and the houses cost about £29 each. The town also appropriated in the same year £30 for schools, and continued to appropriate that amount each year until 1792. Sixty pounds a year was afterwards appropriated for three years or until 1795, when the first mention of "dollars" appears in the town records. A pound at that time appears to have been equivalent to $3.33. In 1797, $300 was appropriated, and the amount was increased from time to time, until in 1823, the sum appropriated for schools was $600.

From that time to the present, the increase in the annual school appropriation has more than kept pace with the growth in population until the present year, when the amount appropriated for schools was $8000.

The inhabitants of the town seem to have "kept the noiseless tenor of their way" for the first fifty years with little to molest or make them afraid. If any important disturbances took place we find no record of them. There was no census until 1765, but we judge from the increase in the number of tax payers, that the growth was simply the slow and steady increase of an exclusively agricultural population. As the land gradually became cleared, it become more thickly dotted with dwellings.

The produce raised upon the farms, and food taken from the river supplied nearly all the wants of the inhabitants. The money necessary for their few purchases, and the payment of taxes, was obtained partly by the sale of wood and timber which was rafted to Newburyport, partly by the production of flax which was sold to the inhabitants of Londonderry, and partly probably by the sale of some unimportant products, such as they could carry on horseback to Salem. They had frequent town meetings every year. Every small matter, such as is now passed upon by the Board of Selectmen, was brought before the whole town, even to the allowance of the smallest order. But the principal town business was the management of religious matters.

In 1729, a committee was chosen to "Discourse with Rev. Christopher Sargent in order to his settlement with us in the work of the ministry." After considerable discussion between Mr. Sargent and the people, it was voted to settle him, giving him as a salary £80 a year, for four years, and then £100 a year so long as he should continue to be their minister. It is an item, worthy of notice—indicating the amount of wood then necessary for a small family,—that Mr. Sargent, at first asked the town to furnish him in addition to his salary 30 cords of wood per year. Mr. Sargent remained pastor for more than fifty years, until old age forced him to resign his charge in 1783. In the eloquent language of one of his successors,* "After laying down his work the good old man lived among his people till his death in 1790, March 20. They buried him in the grave yard on Old Meeting-house hill 'and his sepulchre is with us till this day.' Close to the dear old walls within which for fifty-three years his voice had proclaimed the gospel of peace they laid him. And so it was that on summer days when the windows were open and the sermon went on the straying breeze, it tenderly carried the well loved words from the preachers' lips to his lowly mound, and waved the violets above his head—and the sleeper slept."

In 1774, the inhabitants of the west part of Methuen petitioned to be set off with the easterly part of Dracut to make a new township, "so that both the above said towns may be better accommodated to attend public worship." The proposed line of the new town commenced just east of "Bodwell's ferry" (Tower hill), and ran northwest until it met the Province line one hundred and fifty-six poles west of Splcket river, thus cutting off a large portion of the town. There was a strong opposition on the part of Methuen, and the scheme failed.

About this time we begin to find indications of the coming contest. The first record we find of any action by the town

* Rev. T. G. Grassie.

relative to the questions then stirring the public mind, is a vote passed in August, 1774, to pay one pound, sixteen shillings and seven pence, lawful money, to defray the charges of the Provincial Congress. A little later in the year the town voted in substance, not to pay the province rates, but instead, "That the Selectmen conduct themselves respecting the Constable's Warrants according to the Provincial Congress Instructions."

No other record of any action at that time appears in the regular records of the town, but on one of the last leaves of the book we find the following:

"At a leggel meeting er the freeholders and other Inhabitants of the Town of Methuen held By adjournment from the ninth of August 1774 to the 20th of September 1774.

Taking into Serious Consideration the Stat: of public Affairs, Voted that a Committee be chosen to consult and Advise with Each other Likewise with Committees of other Towns and if need be to communicate to any other Town any mesuers that may appear to be conducive to the publick Benefite more Especlay to be Watch-full that no Encrochments are not made on our Costitutinal Rights and Liberties, that we may enjoy the Blessing we have Left in peace and not be Deprived of them from aney quarter but may Devise prosecute the most vigerous and reseleute mesures as far as Lyes in our sphere retrieve our invaluable privelages. Voted that this Committee consist of fifteen persons.

STEPHEN BARKER Esq.,	JOHN MUSE,
JOHN BODWELL,	JAMES MALLOON,
NATHANIEL PETTENGILL,	JOHN PETTENGILL,
SAMEEL BODWELL,	LIEUT. JOHN SARGENT,
CUTTING MARSH,	RICHARD WHITTIER,
DAVID WHITTIER,	EBENEZER CALTON,
JONATHAN SWAN,	JOHN MASTEN.
JAMES JONES,	

Voted that the above should be entered in the Town Clerks office.

That the people began to contemplate the possibilty of war with Great Britain is indicated by the following, which is an exact copy of the original now in the possession of A. C. Goodell, Esq., of Salem:

"Whareas milartrary Exercise hath been much nelicked We the Subcrbers being the first comptrey in methuen Do Covenant and Engage To from our sevels in to a Bodey in order to Larn the manual Exercise To be Subegat To Such officers as the Comptrey shall chuse by Voat in all constutenel marsher according to our Chattaers.

methuen ye 6th ot octr 1774.

James Jones,
Ichabod Perkins,
James Wilson,
Timothy Eaton,
Ebenezer Colton,
Thomas Runnels,
Henry Morss,
Samuel Messer,
Daniel Messer,
Nathl Haseltine,
Richard Hall,
Samuel Parker,
Stephen Webster, Jr.,
Jacob Messer,
Daniel R. Whittier,
Samuel Webber,
Jacob Hall,
Amos Gage,
John Cross,
Nathan Russ,
Richard Jaques,
Silas Brown,
William Whittier,
John Marsten, Jr.,
Nathaniel Smith Messer,
James Silver, Jun.,
Abiel How,
Timothy Emerson,
Joshua Emerson, Jr.,
Robert Hastings,
James Chase,
Nath. Herrick,
Joseph Hastings,
Kimball Calton,
Richard Currier,
Ebenezer Eaton,
Simeon Hasttins,
John How, Jr.,
Farnum Hall,
Ephraim Clark,
William Runels,
Asa Currier,
Nathaniel Messer,
Ebenezer Messer,
Nathan Perley,
John Keley,
Asa Messer,
John Eaton,
John Davison,
William Stevens,
Simeon Cross,
Francis Swan, Junr,
James Davison,
Jacob How,
Elijah Carlton,
Joseph How,
Jonathan How,
Asa Morss,

Oliver Emerson, Nathl Clark,
Timothy How, John Merrill,
Isaac Barker, Abiel Cross,
Theodore Emerson.

the ferst Compyney in Methuen meat att Mr. Eben Carlton's in order To Chuse officers, and thay chose Lieut. Benj'm Hall Moderator. they Chose Mr. James Jones for thar Capt. Mr. Ichobied Perkins furst Leut. Mr. James Wilson Sonent Leut. Mr. Sam l. Messer Ens. Mr. Nath ll. Messer Jr. Clark for said Compyney.

WILLIAM PAGE Clark for sd. metten.

methuen ye 6 of Octor 1774.

In Jan. 1775, the town voted to give to the poor of the Town of Boston by subscription, and chose a committee to receive the donations. At the same meeting it was voted that minute-men be "drawn out or exposed to train" who should have eight pence per day to the last of March. At the annual meeting in March, it was voted to provide bayonets "which should be brought to Capt. John Davis and after the service was over said Davis is to return said bayonets unto the Selectmen of said town." Soon after the town voted to provide guns for all minute-men unable to furnish themselves, also to provide blankets and cartridges.

Another interesting document, dated about this time, is also found out of place on one of the last leaves of the book or records, as follows:

"We, the subscribers, being appointed a committee by the Town of Methuen to give some instructions to a certain Committee of Safety and Correspondence that was chosen by this town in September last, or may hereafter be chosen, as above, that it is recommended that the above committee do strictly observe and conform to the instructions hereafter mentioned.

First. That you will be vigilant in this time of public distress, that (no) infractions, violations be made on the good and wholesome laws of this province whereby the morals of the people are endangered of being corrupted, and in case you should be unsuccessful in your endeavors in all proper ways, then to publish their names that the public may see and know them to be enemies to their country and the privileges of the same.

Secondly. That you correspond with committees of other towns if you see it needful, as may be necessary on all important occasions.

Thirdly. As a Committee of Inspection, we recommend to you that you will not buy or purchase any British manufactures or superfluities in your families, but such as are of absolute necessity, and likewise that you recommend to others to do the same, for we think that a reformation of this will greatly tend to lessen our private expense and the better enable us to bear the publick charges and prevent those mischiefs that may ensue thereupon.

Fourthly. That you will suppress as much as possible those persons, if any such there be, who travel as pedlers to introduce British goods and impose on the inconsiderate which may impoverish us. And whereas it is said that our enemies are sending out spies in order to get information of our schemes and plans which are contrived for our defense, so as they may frustrate them, it is recommended that you take care that they receive that resentment due to their deeds.

Fifthly. If any trader or other person within this town shall take the advantage of the present distressed circumstances in America, and by an avaricious thirst after gain shall raise the price of any comodity whatsoever beyond their usual, reasonable price, or shall use their influence by words or actions to weaken the measures advised by the Grand Continental Congress, when made to appear to you that he or they persist in the same, you are to publish their names that they may be publickly known and treated as enemies to their country.

JAMES INGALLS,
JONATHAN SWAN, } Committee.
JOHN HUSE,

Methuen, April 4th, 1775.

It will be noticed that this paper was dated about two weeks before the battle of Lexington. It indicates the resolute deliberate earnestness with which our fathers entered the contest, and that our humble ancestors in Methuen were as fully imbued with the spirit of resistance to tyranny as the more widely known men of the time. Our town records are silent in regard to the events at Lexington and Bunker Hill. It probably never occurred to our ancestors that their children would listen to a recital of their actions on those great days, with a feeling of pride such as no other event in our history can arouse.

But fortunately we are not without an official record of the part Methuen had in those great events. The archives at the State House contain the names of those who went from Methuen on the memorable 19th of April, and also the names of the Methuen company who fought at the battle of Bunker Hill. So many Methuen people will take an honest pride in seeing the names of their ancestors included in that roll of honor, that we give the full list of names just as they are found on the original muster rolls now on file in the office of the Secretary of State.

"Capt. John Davis' Company, in Col. Frye's Regt. enlisted Feb. 14th, 1775":

Capt., John Davis	Amos Harramon,
1st Lieut., Nath'l Herrick	Daniel Morse,
2d " Eliphalet Bodwell,	James Ordway,
Sergt., Eleazer Carleton,	Ebenezer Herrick,
" Richard Hall,	Daniel Messer,
" Francis Swan,	Nathan Russ,
" Jona. Barker,	James Ingalls,
Corp'l, Jonathan Baxter,	James Davison,
" William Stevens,	Amos Gage, drummer,
" John Davison,	Joseph Morse,
" Joshua Emerson,	Dudley Noyes,

James Campbell,
Silas Brown,
Enos Kings
Asa Morse,
Eben'r Pingrief,
Simeon Tyler,
Joseph Jackson,
Aaron Noyes,
Parker Bodwell,
Solomon Jennings,
Joshua Bodwell,
Dudley Bailey,
James Silver,
Joseph Hibbard,
Prince Johnnot,
Daniel Jennings,
Wm. Whitcher,
Nathan Swan,
Peter Barker,
Peter Webster,
John Swan,
Daniel Bailey,
Thomas Bace,
Jeremiah Stevens,
Ebenezer Sargent,
John Merrill,
Samuel Barker, Fifer.

This muster roll made for seven days from April 19th.

Sworn to. JOHN DAVIS.

49

" Muster roll of the following number or party of men that belonged to Methuen, in the County of Essex, on the alarm on the 19th of April, 1775, and never joined to any particular commanding officer":

Capt., James Mallon,
Abner Morrill,
Isaac Austin,
Isaac Austin, Jr.,
Benj. Herrick,
Peter Harris,
Joseph Griffin,
Francis Richardson,
Elisha Parker,
John Parker, Jr.,
Isaac Hughs,
Timothy Chellis,
—— Bodwell, 3d,
——Austin, Jr.,
——Parker, Jr.,
Obadiah Morse,
Wm. Russ, Jr.,
Wm McCleary,
Hezekiah Parker,
Jesse Barker,
Moses Morse,
James Dennis.

"The pay roll of the company under the command of Major Samuel Bodwell, exhibited in consequence of the alarm on the 19th of April":

1st Lieut., David Whittier,	John Webber,
2d " Nath. Pettengill,	Benj. Mastin,
Ensign, Enoch Merrill,	Elijah Sargent,
Clerk, John Hughs,	Joshua Stevens,
Sergt., John Mansur,	John Whittier, Jr.,
Wm. Gutterson,	Abel Merrill,
Nath'l Pettengill,	Joseph Morrill,
Thomas Pettengill,	John Richardson,
Dudley Pettengill,	Wm. Richardson,
Daniel Tyler,	Nath'l Hibbard,
John Pettengill, Jr.,	James Hibbard,
Sam'l Cross,	Bodwell Ladd,
John Bodwell,	John Ladd,
Parker Richardson,	Stephen Barker,
Thos. Dow,	Mitchell Davis,
Wm. Bodwell,	Eben'r Barker,
Wm. Morse,	Nehemiah Barker,
John Barker,	Sam'l Richardson,
Simeon Dow,	Enoch Cheney,
Samuel Cole,	Jona. Barker, Jr.,
Samuel Hughs,	Benj. Stevens, J.,
John Pettengill,	John Hibbard, Jr.,

Wm. Hibbard.

45

"Capt. James Jones' pay roll for the campaign on the defence of the country at the battle at Concord, made at the rate of 28 days per month, 4 days' service":

Capt., James Jones,	Isaac Barker,
Lieut., Ichabod Perkins,	Day Emerson,

Sergt., Timothy Eaton,	Joseph Perkins,
" Nathan Perley,	Jona. How,
" Ephraim Clark,	Nath'l S. Clark,
" Jacob Messer,	John Tippets, 3d,
Corp., Nath'l Haseltine,	Oliver Emerson,
" Elijah Carleton,	James Messer,
" Simeon Cross,	Henry Mors,
Drummer, John Kelly,	Stephen Webster, Jr.,
Abiel Cross,	Elisha Perkins,
William Page,	Job Pingrey,
Moses Sargent,	Joseph Cross,
James Fry,	Asa Cross,
Thomas Herrick,	John Morris,
Joseph Granger,	Kimball Carleton.

32

In the Company of Capt. Charles Furbush:

Theodore Emerson,	James Silver,
Isaac Maloon,	John Hancock,
Jos. Pettengill,	Nehemiah Kidah,
Abraham P. Silver,	Daniel Pettengill.

8

Total 156.

The number of inhabitants in Methuen in 1776, according to the Colonial Census, was 1326. The old tax book of that year gives the names of 252 poll tax payers.

Prabably every one will share our own astonishment to find that old Methuen sent 156 men at the first call to meet the British. This would now be equivalent to about 600 men, or more than we see presenr at an annual town meeting. Nothing we have ever heard or read so forcibly impresses us with the universal, deep-seated determination of our fathers to protect their rights, at all hazards, as this simple list of names. No orator has so eloqnently told the story of the popular uprising when Concord and Lexington were attacked. When we consider that they were not called out by any order of the authorities, that their enthusiasm had not been stirred by appeals from the daily press or by public speakers, that they only knew from the signal guns and fires on the hills that the British were in motion, and that nearly every able-bodied man in town, must, of his own accord, have shouldered his musket and marched, at a moment's warning, to meet the foe, we cannot help feeling the blood tingle in our veins with an honest pride in such an ancestry. If this was a sample of the Revolutionary spririt, all wonder ceases that the colonies were successful against such fearful odds.

No other important event took place until the battle of Bunker Hill, on the 17th of June following, in which it is certain that a Methuen company bore an important part. The following is a copy of the original muster roll on file at the State House:

Cambridge, Oct. 5, 1775.

"Return of the men's names, when they enlisted, and where they belonged. Belonging to Capt. John Davis' Company in Col. Frye's Regiment:

Capt., John Davis,	Jeremiah Stevens,
1st Lieut., Nath'l Herrick,	James Silver,
2d " Eliphalet Bodwell,	Simeon Tyler,
Major, Jonathan Barker,	Drummer, Amos Gage,
Serg., Ebenezer Carleton,	Fifer, Samuel Barker,
" Richard Hall,	James Campbell,
" Francis Swan,	James Davison,
" Peter Barker,	Mitchel Davis,
Corp., Jonathan Baxter,	Amos Harriman,
" William Stevens,	Lazarus Hubbard,
" Joshua Emerson,	Ebenezer Herrick,
" John Davison,	Died June 17.

Abraham Anness,	Joseph Hibbard,
John Asten,	Died June 20.
Silas Brown,	James Ingalls,
Parker Bodwell,	Died July 8.
David Bailey,	Dudley Noyes,
Dudley Bailey,	Aaron Noyes,
Timothy Chellis,	Peter Webster,
David Corliss,	James Woodbury,
James Ordway,	Ebenezer Sargent,
Samuel Parker,	Ebenezer Pingrief,
Thomas Pace,	Joshua Bodwell,
Nathan Russ,	In train June 17.
John Swan,	Solomon Jennings,
Nathan Swan,	In train June 17.

47

It is by no means certain that the above list includes the names of *all* Methuen men in the service at that time. It is much to be regretted that our knowledge of the particular part which the Methuen Company had in that battle is so meager. It is known that it was in the thickest of the fight, and that it was among the last to leave the redoubt. It is said that it came near being surrounded towards the end of the battle, and that as the enemy came up on each hand a British soldier ran up to Capt. Davis, saying, "You are my prisoner." Capt. Davis, who was a resolute, powerful man, replied, "I guess not," at the same time running the soldier through with his sword.

The blood spurted over his breeches as he drew back the sword, but he made his escape. It is also said that he took one of his wounded men upon his back just after escaping from the redoubt, and carried him out of the reach of danger. As he was crossing the hollow between the hills, which was exposed to the fire from a British vessel, he saw before him a board fence. Capt. Davis, tired by excitement and the weight of his comrade, said: "I don't see how we can get over that fence." But in an instant after, a cannon ball knocked it in pieces and left the way clear.

There are probably many old stories and traditions of the battle still remembered by the older of our inhabitants, which would be of much interest if collected. Mr. Asa M. Bodwell tells a story of James Ordway, who afterwards lived on the west side of Tower hill:

Mr. Ordway, was in poor circumstances in his old age, and had a bad ulcer on his leg. Mr. Bodwell says that his father sent him one day to Mr. Ordway with a gallon of rum to bathe his lame leg, and with it a message saying that the rum was sent to pay for throwing stones at the battle of Bunker Hill! The story being, that when the ammunition gave out, at the close of the battle, Ordway laid down his gun and threw stones at the British until driven out. It is impossible to imagine the intense anxiety with which our ancestors, who remained at home, must have listened throughout that long summer day, to the roar of artillery, which, tradition says, could be plainly heard. The anxiety must have been two-fold; first to know on which side the victory would rest in the unequal contest, and also whether the booming of the guns which they heard with such terrible distinctness was not the death knell of the dear ones whom they knew were in the fight. Such forebodings were not unfounded, for Methuen lost three men on that day. Ebenezer Herrick was killed in the battle; Joseph Hibbard was wounded and died June 20; James Ingalls was wounded and died July 8.

It is impossible to ascertain the number of soldiers Methuen had in the Revolutionary war, without making a more extended examination of the State records than thé time allowed for the preparation of this paper will admit. The town records give no information on this point, but there is little doubt that Methuen kept her quota in the field. There are stories told in town of events that happened to Methuen men who went to fight Burgoyne, and also to others who were stationed on the coast. During those years the town business went on as usual. Mr. Sargent's salary was voted by the town each year unil 1778, after which we find no record of money raised *by the town* to support the minister. A committee of Safety and Correspondence was appointed each year, and in February, 1778, the town voted that the Selectmen should supply the families of soldiers in the Continental Army with the necessaries of life.

At the same meeting the town was called upon to see what instructions it would give to their Representative, relative to a resolve of the Continental Congress for all the United States of America to join in a perpetual union with one another. The subject was referred to a committee consisting of Major Bodwell, Capt. James Jones, Col. Thomas Poor, Lieut. John Huse and Mr. Enoch Merrill. At an adjourned meeting the question was put whether the town would receive and accept the Articles of Confederation and perpetual union, and "voted in the affirmative." The currency question seems to have troubled our fathers at this time, for we find a vote passed in April, "that those who refuse to take the Continental currency should be treated as enemies, and published in the Boston newspapers." The rapid decrease in value of this currency is shown by the fact, that while in '77 £30 was raised to repair highways, in '81 £6000 was raised for the same purpose.

In 1780, the new Constitution of the State of Massachusetts took effect, and in that year we find the first record of a vote for Governor and Senators. That party feeling did not run very high is evident from the fact that for the office of Governor, John Hancock had sixty-four votes and James Bowdoin, two. The town furnished the equipments for its soldiers and towards the end of the war we find recorded votes to furnish beef and corn.

In the fall of 1780 Methuen furnished 8780 pounds of beef, and hired sixteen men; the next year the town furnishod twelve men. We find nothing in the town records to indicate the end of the war except a vote to sell the entrenching tools belonging to the town. Judging from the census returns, and tax lists, it seems that Methuen grew but little in wealth and population during the forty years subsequent to the Revolutionary war. In the war of 1812, Methuen sent her proportion of men to meet the old enemy. Some of the survivors are with us to this day. Our townsman, Mr. Geo. W. Pecker, one of the veterans of the war, tells us that the number of men called from Methuen was not large. They were mostly stationed to defend the forts along the coast. We are told, however, that a small company went from Methuen to meet the British in Canada, and that they were present at the surrender of Hull.

In 1793, a company was organized to build a bridge over the Merrimack, at Bodwell's falls. Soon after, a meeting was held to see if the town would send a remonstrance to the General Court against its erection. This proposition was decided in the negative. The opponents of the bridge then called a meeting to see if the town would petition the General Court to order the proprietors to pay the cost of the town roads leading to the bridge. This, also, was voted down, and the town decided to repair the road over Currant's hill to New Hampshire line. Up to that time, ferries had furnished the only means of crossing the Merrimack. We find mention of five different ferries, as follows:

"Gage's Ferry," near the house of Samuel Cross.

"Swan's Ferry," at Wingate's farm.

"Marston's Ferry," at the Alms House, Lawrence.
"Bodwell's Ferry," at the Pumping Station, "
"Harris' Férry," a little east of Dracut line.

The Bridge was built shortly after, and for some years the travel from thence to New Hampshire passed over "Currants hill." The "Turnpike" was built in 1805-6, by an incorporated company. A system of toll was established, but it caused such dissatisfaction that in a few years it was made a public road. We are told that, at the beginning of this century, there were only six houses in the now thickly settled part of Methuen Village :—

"The Miller Cross House," corner of Hampshire and Lowell streets.
"Sargent House," where hotel stands.
"Dea. Frye," Butter's place.
"Swan Place," David Nevins' Farm.
"Jona. Cluff House," mill yard.
"John Sargent," at elm tree, by mill yard.

There was then one grist mill, a little south of Fulton's store, another on the opposite side of the river, and a fulling mill just below the foot-bridge at the falls. The first store in town was opened by Abial Howe at a building on Howe St., nearly opposite the house of Charles L. Tozier. The exact date is unknown, but it is within the recollection of persons now living. The town, at that time, and long afterwards was a farming community. Their markets were so far away that their money incomes must have been small. They depended on the city of Salem as a market for their produce, and their wood and timber was rafted to Newburyport.

These two places were the only outlets of importance for their surplus products until after the City of Lowell was started. Then, everything except wood was carried there, and the farmers found the new market greatly for their advantage. Lowell continued to be the principal market for agricultural products until the building of Lawrence furnished a more convenient, and in some respects, better market than Lowell, and gave the farmers of Methuen as good facilities for the successful cultivation of the land, as can be found in any part of New England. Nevertheless, it is a curious fact which we shall not attempt to discuss, that the population of Methuen outside of the village is no larger in 1876 than at the beginning of the Revolutionary war.

From the old traditions, we should judge that the manufacture of hats has been carried on in Methuen from a very early date. No doubt in a very small way at first, but there are several places in the east part of the town pointed out as the site of "hatters' shops." The work was then done entirely by hand, and half a dozen men or less could carry on the whole business of a shop. With the introduction of machinery, the business has been concentrated into a few factories, which have largely increased the production, and now make up a very important portion of the business of the town.

A similar statement would, perhaps, be true of the shoe business. In the early times shoemaking was not carried on to so great an extent as hatting. But within the recollection of many of us, there was a shoemaker's shop in every neighborhood and at nearly every house in town. Shoes were then all made by hand and the workmen took out the stock for a "set" and carried it home to make. In a still summer day it was almost impossible to get away from the noise of the shoemaker's hammer, which sounded like the drumming of a partridge, as he gave the shoe a few final raps after he finished driving the pegs. This business, as every one knows, is now centred in factories where by the use of machinery the manufacture is largely increased. In past times it is probable that more persons have been dependent on the shoe business for a livelihood, than on the manufacture of hats. It is not known precisely when Spicket falls was first utilized as a water power. Mr. Nevins has in his possession a deed from the widow of John Morrill, dated Dec. 1709, in which she conveys to Robert Swan, for the sum of thirty pounds, one-fourth of a sawmill and land "on Spicket river falls, the mill that was built by and belonged to and amongst Robert Swan, John Morrill and Elisha Davis." Without doubt this was the first mill built.

Afterwards a grist mill was built on each side of the river, and, as there was not business enough to keep them both running, it was agreed between them that they should run on alternate weeks. This arrangement was kept up until the cotton factory was built. We are informed that the first cotton factory was built somewhere near 1812 by Stephen Minot, Esq., of Haverhill, on the north side of the river. This was burnt in 1818, and soon after rebuilt. In July, 1821, the whole privilege and lands connected therewith were purchased by the Methuen Company. The old carding or fulling mill which had stood on the south side of the falls, was moved away and converted into a dwelling house, which now stands on the north side of Pelham street. In 1826-7 the brick mill was built as it now stands. In 1864 the property came into the possession of David Nevins, Esq., by whom it has been greatly increased in capacity and value, and to whose enterprise the town is largely indebted for its recent prosperity.

In 1824, a sawmill and gristmill were built where the Methuen woolen mill stands. They came into the possession of Samuel A. Harvey, Esq., by whom the business of the respective mills was carried on for some years. In 1864, a factory was built by the Methuen Woolen Co., and soon after put in operation.

According to the census returns the population increased but little from 1776 until 1820. The building of the cotton mills and increase in the manufacture of shoes and hats, enlarged the business and population of the town so that it gained about seventy per cent. in the next twenty years. During that time there were few events requiring particular notice. In 1837, it appears that a new town house was talked about and a committee was chosen at the March meeting to select location and prepare estimates. The committee reported at an adjournment, and the town voted to build. A week or two afterwards another meeting was called, the vote reconsidered and committee discharged. The same year, the Selectmen were authorized to hire the Baptist meeting-house for holding town meetings. That house continued to be the place for town meetings until the present town house was built, in 1853.

In 1844 rumors began to circulate of a project to dam the Merrimack, and build factories, at Bodwell's falls. The town votéd to give Daniel Saunders and his associates a refusal of the town farm,—which was situated on the east side of Broadway, south of Haverhill street—at its cost, with an addition of thirty-three per cent. The terms on which the Essex Co. bonded the land now occupied by the principal part of Lawrence, were—a fair cash value, with an addition of thirty-three per cent. The land was bought in due time, and the "New City," as it was then called, grew with wonderful rapidity. We are told that there were then only nine or ten houses standing on what is now the thickly-settled part of North Lawrence. A. Durant, had a paper mill on the Spicket, a short distance above its mouth. In 1847 Chas. S. Storrow and others petitioned for an act of incorporation as a new town, to be named Lawrence. A town meeting was called, and the town voted to oppose the division, and chose John Tenney and Geo. A. Waldo to oppose the petition, before the Committee of the

Legislature. Their efiorts were unsuccessful, and Methuen lost a large section of her territory. The publication of a newspaper, called the "Methuen Falls Gazette" was commenced here in January, 1835, by S. J. Varney. It had a short existence, and since then there has been no weekly paper until the publication of the "Transcript" the present year.

Old residents of the town will call to mind many matters of much interest in their day, such as the bickerings about the enforcement of the liquor law, the efforts made to suppress the liqor traffic in Salem, the contests over the dividing lines of school districts, and the building of new roads, but they need not be recited here. From 1850 to 1865 there was little change in population.

In 1860, came the war which laid its hand so heavily on the whole land. The events of that time are so fresh in the memory of every one that it is needless to recount them with minuteness. The first action by the town was taken in April, 1861, when the sum of five thousand dollars was voted for the purpose of arming, equipping and furnishing volunteers. A committee, consisting of the Selectmen, Eben Sawyer, J. P. Flint, John C. Webster and Daniel Currier, was appointed "to disburse the money. In August of that year, the town voted to pay State Aid to the families of volunters according to law. In July, 1862, the town voted to pay a bounty of one hundred dollars to each volunteer when mustered into the United States service. At that time forty-seven men were called for; on the second of August the town held another meeting in which it was voted to pay two hundred dollars in addition to the sum already voted—making three hundred in all—to volunteers when mustered into the service. Immediately after came another order from the President for 300,000 "nine months men." A meeting was at once called to adopt measures to obtain the number required from Methuen. It was voted to pay one hundred and fifty dollars to each nine months man when mustered in and credited to the town. The next call for recruits came in November, 1863, and the town voted "to fill its quota under the call for 300,000 men." It also voted to pay the families of drafted men the same State Aid that was paid to families of volunteers. In May, 1874, the Selectmen were authorized to pay one hundred and twenty-five dollars bounty to volunteers in anticipation of a call from the President for more men. After this time, however, few recruits were mustered in. The volunteers from Methuen were scattered through several different regiments, but the largest number was in Company B, 1st Heavy Artillery, Leverett Bradley, Captain.

The heaviest blow received by Methuen men was in the battle of Spotsylvania, where fifteen were killed and many more wounded. The news that the company from Methuen had suffered heavily in the battle, caused great excitement throughout the town, and a meeting of the citizens was immediately held. Resolutions expressive of sympathy and condolence were passed, and it was voted to send an agent to look after the wounded.

It ought to be mentioned here that the Methuen company held an honorable position in this regiment of eighteen hundred men. At the battle of June 16, the regimental color-bearer was twice shot down. Our well-known townsman, Albert L. Dame, was then given this honorable and dangerous place in the regiment, and had the honor of carrying them to the end of the war, and delivering them up to the State.

The number of men lost by Methuen during the war was fifty-two, exclusive of those serving in the navy. According to Gen. Schouler, the town "furnished three hundred and twenty-five men for the war, which was a surplus of fifty-one over and above all demands. Fifteen were commissioned officers. The whole amount of money appropriated and expended by the town on account of the war, exclusive of State Aid, was $38,651.73. In addition to this amount, $7,500.00 were gratuitously given by individual citizens to aid soldiers' families and encourage recruiting." The total amount of State Aid which has been paid to soldiers and their families in this town up to Feb. 1, 1876, is $43,224.37. There was about a thousand dollars in money raised by fairs and levees, and the ladies of Methuen devoted a great deal of time to work for the soldiers. There were two societies, the Sanitary and Christian Commission which performed a vast amount of work whose value cannot be measured in dollars and cents.

Thus it appears that there must have been paid out in this town, directly on account of the war, more than ninety thousand dollars. As we look back over the record of Methuen in the recent conflict, on the readiness with which our men mustered in the field, and the heartiness with which they were supported by those left at home, we cannot help believing that this generation has proved itself not unworthy its Revolutionary ancestry.

In 1826 or '27, a small fire engine, the "Tiger," was bought, one-half the cost being paid by the Methuen Co., and the other half by Major Osgood, John Davis, Thomas Thaxter, Geo. A. Waldo, and J. W. Carleton. Thomas Thaxter was the first foreman. There is no evidence to show that *the town* had any concern in its management. This was the only protection against fire until 1846, when the Selectmen were authorized to purchase a new fire engine and hose, and erect a house. This engine (the Spiggot) was manned by an active and efficient company, and did good service till 1870, when the steamer, E. A. Straw, was purchased and the "Spiggot" laid aside.

One of the first things done by the old settlers, was to lay out a place to bury their dead. In 1828, the town voted "that there should be a graveyard provided in the town, somewhere near the meeting-house," and chose Wm. Whittier and Joshua Swan to measure and bound out the said graveyard! Their report to the town describes the lot as follows: "Beginning with a small pine tree marked with the letter B, thence running southerly to a pine stump marked with B twenty rods in length, thence to a pine tree marked with a B, north-easterly about six or seven rods in width, and so to another pine tree marked with a B, north-westerly about twenty rods, and so to the bounds first mentioned." This was undoubtedly the north end of the 'old burying-ground" on Meeting-House Hill. In 1803 it was enlarged "on the south side" and a hearse was purchased "for the more convenient solemnization of funerals." In 1772 the Selectmen were ordered to lay out a burying-ground in the west part of the town. They laid out one-fourth of an acre, on land given for the purpose, by Richard Whittier. This yard is still used by citizens, and at the last annual meeting a sum was voted to enlarge it. The burying-ground on Lawrence street was purchased and laid out about 1830. These three burial places comprise those owned by the town. Walnut Grove Cemetery was laid out by an association of individuals in 1853.

As has been already stated, the church and minister were supported by a town tax for many years. The last record of a town appropriation for the support of a minister, was in 1778. The "athadoxt" meeting-house first built, stood on "Meeting-House Hill," near the old burying-ground, and appears to have been the only place for public worship in the town for nearly fifty years.

In 1796, the old house was torn down and a new one built on the same spot. The building of this house seems to have excited much interest throughout the town, and it is a curious fact, illustrating the habits of the time, that it was voted, "That the spectators be given a drink of grog apiece at the raising."

As the village sprung up around Spicket falls, "Meeting House Hill" ceased to be the most central place, and to better accommodate the congregation, it was decided, in 1832, to remove the house to the spot now occupied by the stone meeting-house. It stood there until 1855, when the wooden house was torn down, and the present stone house erected.

In 1766, a second church was organized, with Rev. Eliphaz Chapman, pastor. Soon after the "Second Parish" was formed by act of the Legislature. We understand that under this arrangement every taxable person in town was taxed for the support of the minister, but he paid to the parish instead of the town. The meeting-house is said to have stood near the house of Leonard Wheeler. It was afterwards located near the house of Stephen W. Williams, whence it was removed to Lawrence and afterwards burnt.

The Second Parish existed for half a century—until 1816—when it was united with the First Parish. In 1830 it was again organized, but was again united with the old church and parish. At present there is but one Congregational church in the town.

The next church, in point of age, is the Baptist. From an historical discourse delivered at the semi-centennial celebration of that church and society, we gather the following statements: For many years there had been persons of that faith scattered through the town. It is said that a Baptist church was constituted in the west part of the town some time in the last century, but no records of its formation or subsequent proceedings are to be found. The house in which they worshipped was built about 1778, near the burying-ground west of the Bartlet farm. The number of persons holding that faith increased until 1815, when a church was constituted and steps taken for building a meeting-house. Several sites were contemplated, but it was at last voted to build a "two story meeting-house" on a half-acre lot given by Bailey Davis—where the present house now stands. In 1840 the house was rebuilt on the old site, and stood until Sunday, March 14, 1869, when it took fire, during the morning service, and was totally destroyed. The society erected the house which is now standing, in the following summer, on the old spot. This church is the only one of its denomination in the town.

The Universalist church and society was formed in 1824. For some time previous to the erection of a meeting-house, the congregation held their services in a hall in "Wilson Building." As the society grew in numbers and strength, it built the meeting-house which it now occupies. The house and grounds have, however, been remodeled and much improved in appearance within a few years. This church is the only one of its denomination in the town.

We are informed that the Methodist church was first organized in Methuen in 1833 or '34. For four or five years meetings were held in "Wilson's Hall." A meeting-house was then built, which was occupied a few years and then sold to the town, and used as a school-house. After that time the church held its meetings for many years in the town-house. In 1871 it built a meeting-house at the junction of Lowell and Pelham streets, and is evidently in a prosperous condition. In 1833, or thereabouts, there was an Episcopal church formed in Methuen. Little can be learned about it, and it seems to have had a short existence as an organized body.

Of the social and charitable organizations in town, the Masons and Odd Fellows claim a passing notice. About 1825 Grecian Lodge, F. A. A. M., was formed in Methuen, and seems to have prospered for a time, but in the Anti-Masonic excitement some years after, it surrendered its charter. After Lawrence commenced, the Lodge re-organized under the old charter, but within the limits of Lawrence. John Hancock Lodge was constituted in 1860, and now has 138 members. It holds its meetings in Currier's building.

Hope Lodge, of Odd Fellows, was instituted in 1844, and held its meetings in Currier's building. It surrendered its charter to the Grand Lodge in 1855. The Lodge was re-instated in 1869, and since that time appears to have flourished. It has its meetings in "Corliss' Building," and numbers 110 members.

The growth of the town, and the temper of the times are in some measure indicated by the amount of money raised for municipal purposes. Hence we present the following table. The item of "town charges" does not include appropriations for *special* purposes:

	Ministry.	*Schools.*	*Highway.*	*Town charges.*
1726	£45 & 'diat'	£3-10s		£130
1730	80	Uncertain		60
1740	80	"	£100	80
1750	57	"	11	20
1760	53-7	"	50	30
1770	49-14	"	60	70
1780		500	2000	6000
1790		30	150	100
1800		$ 300	$700	$800
1810		450	1200	700
1820		500	1200	1500
1830		800	1500	1200
1840		1000	1500	2500
1850		1700	1800	3500
1860		2500	1800	3500
1870		7000	3000	10,900
1876		8000	4000	11,050

The period of ten years just ended, has undoubtedly been the most prosperous of any in the town's history. The increase in wealth and population, is shown by the following figures, obtained at the Bureau of Statistics of Labor. The first official census was taken in 1765, hence it is impossible to ascertain the population prior to that time.

Date.	*Population.*			
1765	933	Colonial Census		
1776	1326	"	"	
1790	1297	United States Census		
1800	1253	"	"	"
1810	1181	"	"	"
1820	1371	"	"	"
1830	2006	"	"	"
1840	2251	"	"	"
1850	2538	"	"	"
1860	2566	"	"	"
1865	2576	State		"
1870	2959	United States		"
1875	4205	State		"

INDUSTRIAL STATISTICS, 1875.

MANUFACTURES.

	Number.	*Capital Invested.*	*Value of Goods Manufactured.*
Boots and shoes,	3	$130,000	$420,000
Cotton and jute goods,	1	90,000	609,942
Harnesses,	1	1,000	4,000
Hats, woolen,	3	85,000	610,000
Stoves and tinware,	2	5,500	11,500
Woolen shawls and cloaking,	1	150,000	350,750

OCCUPATIONS.

Blacksmithing	3	1,600	8,400
Butchering,	5	2,600	36,900
Carpentering and joinery,	2	3,500	38,000
Harness and saddle repairing	1	600	600
Hat-tip printing,	1	550	850
Masoning,	1	1,000	10,000
Painting,	3	1,250	5,000
Roofing,	1	500	200
Stone-cutting and dressing,	1	500	2,300
Tinsmithing,	2	3,100	1,500
Watch repairing,	1	300	2,000
Wheelwrighting,	1	1,500	4,000

AGGREGATES.

Manufactures (goods made),	11	461,500	2,006,192
Occupations (work done),	22	17,000	109,750
	33	$478,500	$2,115,942

Value of domestic and agricultural products, 1875, $230,802

The increase in value of the manufactures of Methuen, in ten years, is as follows:

1865	$766.872	Gold at $1.57
1875	2,115,942	Gold at 1.12

These values in gold would be,

1865	$488,453
1875	1,889,234

Thus it appears that the actual value of the manufactures of the town nearly quadrupled during the last ten years. The increase in population, in that time, was 1629, or 64 per cent., a rate of increase greater than that of any other town in Massachusetts.

When the census was taken in 1875, it was found that there were about 3000 inhabitants in Methuen village, showing that the increase in population was in the manufacturing, rather than the agricultural part of the town.

The following figures, taken from the valuation books, show the changes in different classes of taxable property for ten years:

	1865.	*1870.*	*1876.*
Polls,	651	880	1,101
Real estate,	$954,963	$1,261,077	$1,709,900
Personal estate,	308,084	543,250	600,870
Total tax,	24,849.80	33,415.67	37,511.57
Rate per thousand,	18.81	17.35	15.30
No. dwelling-houses,	455	519	649
No. horses,	262	319	447
No. cows,	645	722	907
No. sheep,	106	18	6

No. of acres taxed in town, 13,283.

From these statistics it will be seen at once that we have of late been passing through a remarkable period of material growth. There has been no great *speculative* rise in the value of property, and no such depreciation within a year or two, as is almost universal throughout the country. The variety of manufaciuring interests in the town, the proximity to Lawrence, and close connection by the horse railroad—which has been in operation since 1867—have combined to prevent that utter stagnation in business which is so severely felt in many manufacturing towns. Within a year, about twenty dwelling-houses have been built, and nearly ten thousand dollars expended in special public improvements.

We have thus given an imperfect outline of the history of Methuen, to the present time, and close our sketch with the full knowledge that much of interest has been omitted.

Had there been sufficient opportunity we should have been glad to collect and record more of the old legends of the early days, and to have ascertained more facts in relation to our Revolutionary soldiers. It would also have been interesting to trace the history of the men who have been prominent in guiding the affairs, and influencing the character of the town, for the last century and a half. But, as was said in the outset, the time allotted to examine records and prepare this paper, has not permitted a more perfect or extended history than is here given.

We submit it to the charitable consideration of the reader in the hope that it will be estimated by what has been done, regardless of what is omitted.

www.ingramcontent.com/pod-product-compliance
Lightning Source LLC
LaVergne TN
LVHW011121110826
845150LV00008B/2210
* 9 7 8 1 4 1 8 1 9 9 0 0 5 *